FRANCHISING IN VIETNAM 2014

Legal and Business Considerations

KENDAL H. TYRE, JR., EXECUTIVE EDITOR
DIANA VILMENAY-HAMMOND, MANAGING EDITOR
PIERCE HAESUNG HAN, ASSISTANT EDITOR

LEXNOIR FOUNDATION

FOURTH QUARTER 2014

LexNoir Foundation is the charitable, educational arm of LexNoir, an international network of lawyers connecting the African Diaspora.

www.lexnoir.org

Table of Contents

Page

Bibliography of International Franchise Resources

Kendal H. Tyre, Jr., Diana Vilmenay-Hammond, Pierce Haesung Han and Keri McWilliams
NIXON PEABODY LLP

Acknowledgment

This book could not have been written without the hard work and dedication of each of the contributing authors and editors. Thank you.

We would like to acknowledge and extend our heartfelt gratitude to Maria Stallings of the Washington, D.C. office of Nixon Peabody LLP for her invaluable assistance in revising, proofing, and editing this publication.

About the Editors and Authors

Kendal H. Tyre, Jr. – Kendal is a partner in the Washington, D.C. office of Nixon Peabody LLP. He handles domestic and cross-border transactions, including mergers and acquisitions, joint ventures, strategic alliances, licensing, and franchise matters.

In his franchise and licensing practice, Kendal counsels domestic and international franchisors, franchisees, licensors, licensees and distributors regarding U.S. state and federal franchise laws as well as foreign franchise legislation in a variety of jurisdictions. Kendal drafts and provides advice with regard to franchise and license agreements, disclosure documents and area development agreements and has extensive experience drafting and negotiating a variety of other commercial agreements. His client base spans the United States and foreign countries, including South Africa, Kenya, and the United Kingdom.

Kendal is a frequent contributor to franchise publications and a frequent speaker at franchise programs held by the American Bar Association Forum on Franchising and the International Franchise Association.

Kendal is co-chair of the firm's Diversity Action Committee and its Africa Group. Kendal is also the executive director of LexNoir Foundation.

E-mail address: ktyre@nixonpeabody.com

Diana Vilmenay-Hammond – Diana is an attorney in the Washington, D.C. office of Nixon Peabody LLP. She is a member of the firm's Franchise & Distribution team.

In her franchise practice, Diana works with domestic and international franchisors on transactional and litigation matters. Specifically, she counsels franchisor clients regarding state and federal franchise laws, disclosure and registration obligations. Diana drafts and negotiates various commercial agreements, including international franchise and development agreements.

Diana has co-authored numerous articles on franchising and frequently co-hosted the Nixon Peabody franchise law webinar series. Topics have included:

- "Franchise Case Law Round-Up: Implications for Your Franchise;"
- "Social Media Part II: Best Practices in Protecting Your Brand in the New Media;" and
- "The Awuah Case: Bellwether or Outlier."

Diana received her J.D. from Howard University School of Law and her B.A. from Georgetown University. She is a member of the American Bar Association (Forum on Franchising).

E-mail address: dvilmenay@nixonpeabody.com

Pierce Haesung Han – Pierce is an associate in Nixon Peabody's Global Business & Transactions group. Pierce focuses his practice on three main areas, assisting clients with a variety of complex business transactions:

- Mergers & Acquisitions: Providing assistance to both public and private clients with various mergers and acquisitions, performing due diligence, drafting and negotiating transaction documents, and facilitating closing and post-closing mechanics.
- International Commercial Transactions: Drafting and negotiating a variety of commercial agreements, including international franchise and development

agreements, license agreements, and purchase and sale agreements.

- Federal Securities Law Matters: Assisting public and private clients regarding federal securities laws and stock exchange rules relating to corporate governance and disclosure.

Pierce received his J.D. from Georgetown University Law Center and his B.A. from Case Western Reserve University. He is admitted to practice in the State of New York and the District of Columbia.

E-mail address: phan@nixonpeabody.com

Keri McWilliams – Keri is an associate in the Franchise & Distribution team of Nixon Peabody LLP. Keri works with clients on a number of franchising issues, including obtaining and maintaining franchise registrations in various states, responding to state inquiries regarding trade practices, ongoing compliance with state and federal regulations, and updating franchise disclosure documents. She also handles franchise sales counseling and franchise system issues.

Keri is a member of the American Bar Association's Forum on Franchising, and the Federal and Minnesota State bar associations. She is also a member of Minnesota Women Lawyers and the Minnesota Association of Black Lawyers, and a volunteer in the Volunteer Lawyers Network.

Keri received her J.D. from Georgetown University Law Center and her B.F.A. from Washington University. She is admitted to practice in the District of Columbia and Minnesota.

E-mail address: kmcwilliams@nixonpeabody.com

Mai Thi Minh Hang – Hang is a partner at Russin & Vecchi in Hanoi, Vietnam. Hang's practice areas include banking, finance, telecommunications and mining, capital markets, and foreign investment. She has advised offshore clients who want to franchise their businesses in Vietnam. She assists a wide variety of clients on all aspects of business operation in Vietnam, including distribution in the form of direct selling. She assisted the Ministry of Industry and Trade in drafting regulations to implement the Commercial Code, which included government decrees on franchising and direct selling. She has published several articles on franchising and direct selling.

Hang received a B.A. in Economics from Hanoi Foreign Trade University in 1997 and a LL.B. from Hanoi University of Law in 2001. Hang then attended Washington State University to receive an M.B.A. in 2003. Hang speaks Vietnamese and English.

E-mail address: mtmhang@russinvecchi.com.vn

Ngo Viet Hoa – Hoa is an associate at Russin & Vecchi in Hanoi, Vietnam. Hoa's practice areas include corporate, commercial, and foreign investment. He has assisted clients on franchising, export, import and distribution.

Before joining Russin & Vecchi, Hoa worked for the Ministry of Industry and Trade in Vietnam ("MOIT"), as the director of Commercial Law Division. Hoa participated in drafting the Commercial Law 2005 and governmental decrees and ministerial circulars on franchising and distribution. He also took part as a legal advisor in negotiation of free trade agreements between Vietnam and its partners. Currently, although working with Russin & Vecchi, Hoa continues to provide comments on draft laws and regulations at the request of the MOIT and the Vietnam Chamber of Commerce and Industry.

Hoa received a LL.B. from Hanoi University of Law in 2002 and a LL.M. from the University of Melbourne Law School in 2009. Hoa speaks Vietnamese and English.

E-mail address: nvhoa@russinvecchi.com.vn

About the Book

Franchising in Vietnam 2014: Legal and Business Considerations contains excerpts from the larger work *Franchising in Asia 2014: Legal and Business Considerations*. Both books serve as practical, succinct, easy-to-use reference tools for lawyers, business people and academics to use in navigating the laws and business issues impacting franchise arrangements in Asia.

This book provides an overview of the franchise industry in Vietnam and addresses the typical legal issues confronted when expanding a franchise system in Vietnam. The larger work, *Franchising in Asia 2014: Legal and Business Considerations*, covers those laws governing franchising in several other Asian countries.

In both books, an author, who is a legal expert in the designated jurisdiction, addresses the basic questions that a franchise lawyer would need to know to competently represent a client in expanding their franchise system to that country.

Each country chapter organizes a discussion of that country's laws under various headings and in a uniform format. Topics were sent to each country's author in the form of a questionnaire, and each author drafted responses to the questions presented. A general overview relating to the political and economic history of the country at the beginning of each chapter provides an initial context for the regulatory framework.[1]

---

1 The source of information for these sections is the Central Intelligence Agency, https://www.cia.gov/library/publications/the-world-factbook/ (last visited November 5, 2014).

Apart from an overview of the legal framework for franchising, each book contains other articles and resources that should prove useful to those in the franchise industry.

The authors for each chapter are listed at the beginning of a chapter and their biographical information is listed in the previous section, *About the Editors and Authors*.

Readers should always consult with local counsel in the relevant jurisdiction instead of relying solely on the information contained in this book. The laws governing franchising are evolving and local counsel in Vietnam are best positioned to provide timely, relevant advice applying the current law to the particular facts of a case.

Franchising in Vietnam

Mai Thi Minh Hang and Ngo Viet Hoa
RUSSIN & VECCHI
Hanoi, Vietnam

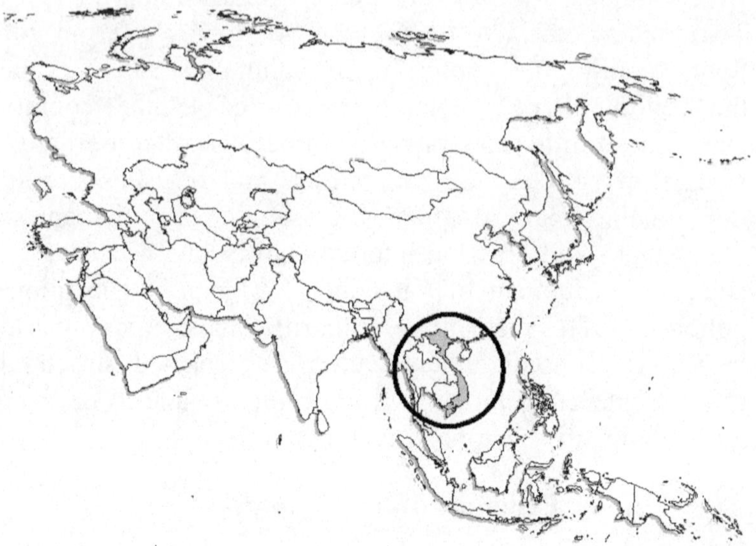

I. Introduction

A. Historical Background of the Country

Vietnam declared independence from France after World War II, but France continued to rule until its 1954 defeat by communist forces under Ho Chi Minh. Under the Geneva Accords of 1954, Vietnam was divided into the communist North and anti-communist South. U.S. economic and military aid to South Vietnam grew through the 1960s in an attempt to bolster the government, but U.S. armed forces were withdrawn following a cease-fire agreement in 1973. Two years later, North Vietnamese forces overran the South reuniting the country under communist rule. Despite the return of peace, for over a decade the country experienced little economic growth because of conservative leadership policies, the persecution and mass exodus of individuals - many of them successful South Vietnamese merchants - and growing international isolation. However, since the enactment of Vietnam's "*doi moi*" (renovation) policy in 1986, Vietnamese authorities have committed to increased economic liberalization and enacted structural reforms needed to modernize the economy and to produce more competitive, export-driven industries.

B. Economy of the Country

Vietnam is a densely-populated developing country that has been transitioning from the rigidities of a centrally-planned economy since 1986. Vietnamese authorities have reaffirmed their commitment to economic modernization in recent years. Vietnam joined the World Trade Organization in January 2007, which has promoted more competitive, export-driven industries. Vietnam became an official negotiating partner in the Trans-Pacific Partnership Trade Agreement in 2010. Agriculture's share of economic output has continued to shrink from about 25% in 2000 to less than 20% in 2013, while industry's share increased from 36% to more than 42% in the same period. State-owned enterprises account for about 40% of GDP. Poverty has declined significantly, and Vietnam is working to create jobs to meet the challenge of a labor force that is growing by more than one million people every year. The global recession hurt Vietnam's export-oriented economy, with GDP in 2013 growing at 5%, the slowest rate of growth since 1999. In 2013, however, exports increased by more than 12%, year-on-year; several administrative actions brought the trade deficit back into balance. Between 2008 and 2011, Vietnam's managed currency, the dong, was devalued in excess of 20%, but its value remained relatively stable in 2013. Hanoi has oscillated between promoting growth and emphasizing macroeconomic stability in recent years. In February 2011, the government shifted from policies aimed at achieving a high rate of economic growth, which had stoked inflation, to those aimed at stabilizing the economy, through tighter monetary and fiscal control. Although Vietnam unveiled a broad, "three pillar" economic reform program in early 2012, proposing the restructuring of public investment, state-owned enterprises, and the banking sector, little perceptible progress has been made. Vietnam's economy continues to face challenges from an undercapitalized banking sector. Non-performing loans weigh heavily on banks and businesses.

C. Franchise Legal Overview

The basic regulations on franchising are provided in the Commercial Law, adopted by the National Assembly on June 14, 2005 ("Commercial Law"). These regulations are elaborated on in *Decree No. 35/2006/ND-CP* of the Government (March 31, 2006) ("Decree 35") as amended by *Decree No. 120/2011/ND-CP* of the Government (December 16, 2011) ("Decree 120"), and *Circular No.*

09/2006/TT-BTM of the Ministry of Trade (May 25, 2006) ("Circular 09"). Regulations related to franchising can also be found in the *Law on Intellectual Property*, adopted by the National Assembly on November 29, 2005, and the *Law on Technology Transfer*, adopted on November 29, 2006.

II. Regulatory Requirements

Vietnamese franchise laws apply to franchising activities between Vietnamese parties, to a foreign franchisor who grants a franchise to a franchisee in Vietnam, and to a Vietnamese franchisor who grants a franchise to a franchisee in a foreign country.

A. Pre-sale Disclosure

Please describe any pre-sale franchise disclosure or similar requirements that may apply to franchise transactions.

1. Initial Disclosure

Under *Decree 35*, an information disclosure document titled "Franchise Description Document" (the "FDD") must be submitted to the Ministry of Industry and Trade (the "MOIT") as part of its registration dossier (discussed below). The FDD must be prepared according to a standard form provided by the MOIT under *Circular 09*.

The contents of the FDD must include:

- Information about the franchisor, including: the franchisor's name, address of head office, incorporation date, scope of business, type of business to be franchised, and a description of the organizational structure of the franchisor, including the department that is in charge of the franchising activities of the franchisor;

- Whether the franchisor is the master franchisor or a subfranchisor (master franchisee);
- Litigation history related to franchising activities;
- Initial costs payable by the franchisee;
- Other financial obligations of the franchisee;
- Initial investment by the franchisee;
- Information on trademarks and service marks that will be used in association with the franchised business;
- Obligations of the franchisee to buy or lease equipment as designated by the franchisor;
- Obligations of the franchisor, including: obligations prior to the execution of the franchise agreement; obligations during the course of operation of the franchise system; obligations to consider the franchisee's proposed premises for the franchised business; and obligations to provide training, including initial training, and other training programs;
- Description of the market of the goods/services to be franchised;
- A summary of the franchise agreement;
- Information on the franchise system, including: number of outlets, both currently in operation and those that have ceased to operate; number of franchise agreements the franchisor has signed with franchisees; the number of franchise agreements that have been transferred by franchisees to third parties; the number of franchise agreements that have been terminated or renewed;
- Financial statements of the franchisor; and
- Information on awards or recognition that the franchisor may have received;

Decree 35 also requires the franchisor to provide the franchisee or master franchisee (a franchisee with the right to act as a subfranchisor by granting a franchise to a subfranchisee) with the above FDD and a copy of the franchise agreement at least 15 working days prior to the execution of the franchise agreement.

If a master franchisee wishes to grant a franchise to a subfranchisee, the master franchisee must comply with the disclosure requirements as if it were the franchisor. The master franchisee must also provide a subfranchisee with the contents of the Master Franchise Agreement (the "MFA") and information about the franchisor. It must also inform a subfranchisee of legal remedies in the case the MFA is terminated.

If a foreign franchisor grants a master franchise to a local master franchisee, the foreign franchisor is not required to provide disclosure to local subfranchisees. This is the responsibility of the local master franchisee.

2. Ongoing disclosure

Besides the initial disclosure requirement mandated in the FDD, a franchisor is required to keep its franchisees updated concerning all significant changes related to its franchise system. A "significant change" is defined to be any change that may have an impact on the business activities of a franchisee.

Circular 09 requires the franchisor to report to the MOIT any change in: (a) the name of the franchisor; (b) address of the head office; (c) telephone and fax number; (d) scope of business; or (e) type of business to be franchised. The report must be made within 30 days from the date on which the change occurs.

B. Government Approvals, Registrations, and Filing Requirements

Please describe any necessary government approvals or similar requirements that may apply to franchise transactions.

1. Offshore franchisors

An offshore franchisor must register its franchising activity and file it with the MOIT. The registration dossier must include: (1) a registration form of the franchising activity, made on a standard form provided in *Circular 09*; (2) the FDD; (3) a certified copy of the franchisor's business registration; and (4) a certified copy of patents and certificates of intellectual property rights of the prospective franchisor, if any. If any of these documents are in a foreign language, a certified translation into Vietnamese into Vietnamese is required. The fee to register a franchise is VND 16,500,000 (equivalent to about US$810.00)

If the applicant is a master franchisee, the above dossier must include a document issued by the franchisor that shows permission to subfranchise the business.

The franchising agreement itself need not be included in the dossier unless it is necessary to register the licensing of intellectual property rights that are associated with a franchised business and that fall within the regulations on intellectual property. *See Section V* (Trademarks) on licensing regulations under the *Law on Intellectual Property*.

The MOIT has discretion to determine whether the documentation filed to register the franchising activity meets disclosure requirements. If the MOIT finds the documentation to be incomplete or invalid, it must provide written notice to the applicant that it needs to supplement the necessary documents in order to complete the registration. The applicant has the right to request that the MOIT clarify what additional materials the applicant must provide.

If the registration dossier is approved, *Circular 09* stipulates that the MOIT will register the franchising activity within 5 working days. In practice, however, the time frame can be as long as a month.

2. Vietnamese franchisors

A Vietnamese franchisor, whether it grants a franchise to a foreign or domestic franchisee, is not required to register its franchising activity with the MOIT. Instead, it must report its franchising activity to the provincial Services of Industry and Trade (the "SOITs"). There is no specific provision under *Decree 120* that specifies the content of the report, nor the procedure by which the report is filed. Thus, the report requirement currently appears not to be fully operational.

C. Limits of Fees and Typical Term of Franchise Agreement

Please describe any limits upon the nature and extent of fees and the term of a typical franchise agreement.

The law imposes no limits relating to the nature and extent of fees in a franchisee agreement. Similarly, there are no limits in regards to the duration of a franchise agreement. As such, a franchisor and franchisee may freely negotiate the terms and conditions of a franchise agreement. Decree 35 gives some suggested terms and conditions which can be used for reference, but it is not compulsory to include them in the franchisee agreement.

III. Currency

If all payments under a franchise agreement must be made in immediately available U.S. Dollars, please advise as to any restrictions, reporting requirements, or regulations concerning the exchange, repatriation or remittance of U.S. Dollars.

Generally, there is no exchange control issue in a franchise arrangement. In particular, *Article 6* of the *Ordinance on Foreign Exchange* provides that all payments and money remittances in relation to "current transactions" (including payment for imported goods/services) between a resident and a non-resident may be freely conducted. The remittance of franchise fees by a Vietnamese franchisee to a foreign franchisor is treated as a current transaction, which is freely conducted. Of course, a commercial bank will examine relevant papers and documents in accordance with regulations of the State Bank of Vietnam before it wires money.

IV. Taxes, Tariffs and Duties

Please do not provide any in-depth comments on tax structuring. However, please provide your general comments on the typical amount of withholding tax that would apply and whether a "gross-up" provision contained in a franchise agreement would be enforceable in your country.

Under *Circular No.60/2012/TT-BTC* of the Ministry of Finance dated April 12, 2012 ("Circular 60"), an offshore franchisor is subject to withholding taxes which include value added tax ("VAT") and corporate income tax ("CIT"). Because the offshore franchisor usually is a nonresident and does not have a permanent establishment in Vietnam, the Vietnamese franchisee is generally responsible for the payment of VAT and CIT incurred by the offshore franchisor.

1. CIT

CIT applies to the offshore franchisor's income generated from royalty fees at a rate of 10%. As a matter of practice, income from services, including development and initial franchise fees may be subject to a CIT rate of 5%.

2. VAT

VAT applies to services provided by the offshore franchisor to the Vietnamese franchisee. The amount of VAT that applies to such services is equal to 50% [2] of the revenue that is received by that offshore franchisor before netting of any taxes, multiplied by the VAT rate of 10%.

Under the VAT law, VAT does not apply to royalties the offshore franchisor receives from the Vietnamese franchisee.

3. Double Taxation Relief

An offshore franchisor may find taxation relief under an applicable double taxation agreement ("DTA"), if any. Currently, Vietnam has double taxation treaties in effect or signed with numerous countries (64 total). Of note, however, is that Vietnam currently does not have a DTA signed with the United States.

4. "Gross-up" Provisions

There is currently no law precluding the enforceability of a gross-up provision within a franchise agreement. However, because the Vietnamese franchisee is generally responsible

---

[2] 50% is the percentage of added value assigned for services.

to register, declare, and make payment of CIT and VAT incurred by the offshore franchisor, such a provision would pose an enormous financial burden on the franchisee and likely render the franchise agreement impracticable.

V. Trademarks

Please advise us as to whether there are any special requirements for granting a valid trademark license, including the use of a registered user agreement or a short trademark license agreement and any required filing of such an agreement with the trademark authorities.

A non-resident franchisor must register its trademark in Vietnam for its trademark to be recognized by law. However, an agreement to license the right to use a legally recognized trademark (a trademark licensing agreement) need not be registered with any authority for it to be effective. Nevertheless, the parties to such a licensing agreement may wish to register such an agreement with the National Office of Intellectual Property ("NOIP"), as registration will protect the trademark from a third party's claim.

VI. Restrictions on Transfer

Please advise as to whether there are any restrictions (1) on a franchisor to restrict transfers by a master franchisee, or the assets of the master franchisee, or (2) the ability of a master franchisee to control and/or restrict transfers of a subfranchisee's rights under a master franchise agreement, an interest in the subfranchisee, or the assets of the subfranchisee.

Decree 35 contains no restrictions on the franchisor's ability to restrict transfers by a master franchisee. Similarly, *Decree 35* contains no restrictions on the ability of a master franchisee to control or restrict transfers of a subfranchisee's rights under a master franchise agreement, an interest in the subfranchisee, or the assets of the subfranchisee.

VII. Termination

Please advise us as to any laws relating to the termination in your country, such as agency laws, required indemnity provision, notice or "good cause" requirements, or other laws affecting termination of a franchise agreement. Please describe.

As a matter of background, a franchise agreement is listed as a commercial contract under the *Commercial Law*. The right to unilaterally terminate a commercial contract is generally set out in the *Commercial Law*. In particular, a party to a contract can unilaterally terminate a contract if:

(i) the other party commits a breach of the contract of a type that the parties agreed to be grounds for the non-default party to terminate the contract; or

(ii) there was a material breach of contract by the other party. A material breach is defined as a breach that causes damages to the non-defaulting party such that the non-defaulting party is unable to achieve the purposes of the contract. Due to this qualitative approach, it is therefore up to the courts or arbitrators to decide whether there was a material breach by a party on a case-by-case basis.

In addition, *Decree 35* specially provides for the right of either a franchisee or franchisor to unilaterally terminate a franchise agreement in certain circumstances, as follows:

A franchisee may unilaterally terminate a franchise agreement if the franchisor fails to:

- provide to the franchisee guiding documents on the franchise system;
- provide initial training and regular technical assistance;
- design the operating premises of the franchisee;
- ensure the intellectual property rights of subject matters of the franchise agreement; or
- treat franchisees in its franchising system fairly and equally.

A franchisor may unilaterally terminate a franchise agreement if the franchisee:

- fails to maintain the Business Registration Certificate ("BRC") or other equivalent certificate that is required by law to operate the franchised business;
- is insolvent or dissolved;
- commits a material violation of the law that may cause significant damage to the prestige of the franchising system; or
- fails to remedy, in a reasonable time, a minor breach of a franchise agreement upon the receipt of the franchisor's written notification of such breach.

VIII. Governing Law, Jurisdiction and Dispute Resolution

A. Choice of Law of Foreign Jurisdiction

Please confirm whether the choice of law of a foreign jurisdiction would likely to be upheld under the laws of the country, except for the certain matters such as trademarks, bankruptcy and competition matters, which will assume would be governed in your country.

The choice that a foreign law is to govern a transaction in which one of the parties is a foreign party, is generally permissible, pursuant to the Civil Code and the *Commercial Law*, but subject to certain general conditions. One such condition holds that the application, or the consequence of such application of foreign law, must not be contrary to the basic principles of Vietnamese law. There would, however, only be narrow grounds for challenging a choice of foreign law on the basis that such condition has not been satisfied.

The choice of which law should govern the franchise agreement depends on which venue is chosen to settle a dispute under the franchisee agreement. If the franchise agreement refers a dispute to a venue in Vietnam, either to Vietnamese courts or Vietnamese arbitrators, then a foreign law cannot be the governing law of the franchise agreement. This is simply because, as a matter of practice, the Vietnamese courts and Vietnamese arbitrators may not have sufficient expertise or knowledge on such foreign law to interpret the franchise agreement properly.

B. International Arbitration Dispute Resolution

Please confirm a court in your country would honor an election of international arbitration dispute resolution, and therefore refuse to hear any dispute arising under the franchise agreement.

Vietnam is a signatory to the 1958 New York *Convention on the Recognition and Enforcement of Foreign Arbitral Awards* (the "New York Convention").

Under Vietnamese law, arbitration is acceptable as the exclusive remedy for resolving disputes, except for those disputes that are specified in the Civil Procedure Code to be subject to the exclusive jurisdictions of the courts. The disputes that would arise from a franchise agreement do not fall within the exclusive jurisdiction of the courts and can thus be referred to arbitrators. If the parties agree under the franchise agreement to refer disputes to arbitration, neither party may initiate a court claim.

IX. Non-competition provision

If the franchise agreement prohibits the franchisee from engaging in certain competitive activities during the term of the agreement, and for a 12 month period after the termination or expiration of the agreement, please comment on the enforceability of non-competition covenants in your country.

A non-competition clause in a franchise agreement is permissible under Vietnamese law as a matter of freedom of contract.

However, in practice it would be difficult to enforce such a clause. In particular, the only action that a franchisor can take to prevent the franchisee from engaging in competitive activities is to seek a court's injunctive relief. However, it is not always convenient to do so. This is because the franchisor must have evidence that the franchisee is going to engage in such activities. Such evidence is not easily obtained.

Furthermore, when the competitive activities have already been completed, the franchisor can only rely on remedies for breach of the franchise agreement.

Injunctive relief is available under the Civil Procedure Code to:

- address an urgent request of the claimant;
- protect evidence; or

- prevent the occurrence of a serious consequence.

An injunctive relief can be sought only after the applicant has initiated a petition to the court, a petition to the arbitrator, or together with filing of a petition to the court in respect of a breach of the party against whom the injunctive relief is sought.

The applicant must file a request for an injunctive relief with the court with which the petition is filed, or, if the petition is made to the arbitrator, the court of the province in which the arbitrator sits. An application must address the following matters:

(i) name, address of the applicant and the party against whom the injunctive relief is sought;

(ii) summary of the dispute or breach of the party against whom the injunctive relief is sought ;

(iii) the grounds for the request; and

(iv) the specific measures needed to be taken.

A court must decide whether to grant injunctive relief within 48 hours in cases of extreme urgency, and generally, within three days of receiving the request. An injunctive relief, if granted, must be sent to a competent Department of Civil Judgment Execution for enforcement.

X. Language Requirements:

Does the law in your country require that a franchise agreement be translated into the local language in order to be enforceable between the parties?

The law of Vietnam requires that all franchise agreements to be made in the Vietnamese language. The regulator has explained that this requirement has been included because many local franchisees are small- and medium-size entrepreneurs who are not familiar with foreign languages. A franchising agreement made in Vietnamese is intended to ensure that a local franchisee thoroughly understands and properly performs the agreement, and to avoid disputes due to misinterpretation. This language restriction, however, does not apply to a franchise agreement under which a Vietnamese franchisor grants a franchise in a foreign country.

XI. Other significant matter:

Please advise as to whether there are any significant matters not addressed above of which a franchisor should be aware in connection with its entering into a franchise agreement in your country.

There are no other significant matters to be addressed.

Bibliography of International Franchise Resources

Kendal H. Tyre, Jr., Diana Vilmenay-Hammond,
Pierce Haesung Han and Keri McWilliams
NIXON PEABODY LLP
Washington, D.C.

I. General International Resources

Mark Abell, Gary R. Duvall, and Andrea Oricchio Kirsh, *International Franchise Legislation* B1, ABA FORUM ON FRANCHISING (1996)

Kathleen C. Anderson and Anthony M. Stiegler, *Put Muscle in Your Marks: Enforcing Intellectual Property Rights* W14, ABA FORUM ON FRANCHISING (1995)

Richard M. Asbill and Jane W. LaFranchi, *International Franchise Sales Laws—A Survey* W7, ABA FORUM ON FRANCHISING (2005)

Jeffery A. Brimer, Alison C. McElroy, and John Pratt, *Going International: What Additional Restraints Will You Face?* W4, ABA FORUM ON FRANCHISING (2011)

Michael G. Brennan, Alexander Konigsberg, and Philip F. Zeidman, *Globetrotting: A Workshop on International Franchising* 10/W8, ABA FORUM ON FRANCHISING (1994)

Michael G. Brennan, Alexander Konigsberg, and Philip F. Zeidman, *Globetrotting: Strategies for Launching U.S.*

Franchisors Abroad 2/P2, ABA FORUM ON FRANCHISING (1994)

Christopher P. Bussert and Jennifer Dolman, *Regaining Your Trademark After Abandonment or Misappropriation* W7, ABA FORUM ON FRANCHISING (2011)

Ronald T. Coleman and Linda K. Stevens, *Trade Secrets and Confidential Information: Rights and Remedies* W2, ABA FORUM ON FRANCHISING (2000)

Finola Cunningham, *Commerce Department Helps Franchisors Go Global*, in FRANCHISING WORLD 63 (Dec. 2005)

Michael R. Daigle and Alex S. Konigsberg, *Meeting Off-Shore Disclosure and Contract Requirements* F/W13, ABA FORUM ON FRANCHISING (1992)

Jennifer Dolman, Robert A. Lauer, and Lawrence M. Weinberg, Structuring International Master Franchise Relationships for Success and Responding When Things Go Awry W22, ABA FORUM ON FRANCHISING (2007)

Gary R. Duvall, Paul Jones, and Jane LaFranchi, *Planning for the International Enforcement of Franchise Agreements* W6, ABA FORUM ON FRANCHISING (1999)

William Edwards, International Expansion: Do Opportunities Outweigh Challenges? in FRANCHISING WORLD (February 2008)

George J. Eydt and Stuart Hershman, *Bringing a Foreign Franchise System to the United States* W9, ABA FORUM ON FRANCHISING (2009)

William A. Finkelstein and Louis T. Pirkey, *International Trademarks* W15, ABA FORUM ON FRANCHISING (1991)

William A. Finkelstein, Protecting Trademarks Internationally: Current Strategies and Developments B3, ABA FORUM ON FRANCHISING (1996)

Stephen Giles, Lou H. Jones, and Lawrence Weinberg, *Negotiating and Documenting Complex International Franchise Agreements* W21, ABA FORUM ON FRANCHISING (2006)

Steven M. Goldman, Stephen Giles, Marc Israel, and Stanley Wong, *Competition Round Up from Around the World* LB2, ABA FORUM ON FRANCHISING (2004)

David C. Gryce and E. Lynn Perry, *Trademarks and Copyrights in the International Arena* 6/W4, ABA FORUM ON FRANCHISING (1993)

Kenneth S. Kaplan, Andrew P. Loewinger, and Penelope J. Ward, *System Standards in International Franchising* W14, ABA FORUM ON FRANCHISING (2005)

Edward Levitt and Jorge Mondragon, A Survey of International Legal Traps and How to Avoid Them—Beyond the Franchise Laws W20, ABA FORUM ON FRANCHISING (2007)

Ned Levitt, Kendal H. Tyre, and Penny Ward, *The Impossible Dream: Controlling Your International Franchise System* W4, ABA FORUM ON FRANCHISING (2010)

Michael K. Lindsey and Andrew P. Loewinger, *International (Non-U.S.) Franchise Disclosure Requirements* W9, ABA FORUM ON FRANCHISING (2002)

Andrew P. Loewinger and John Pratt, *Recent Changes and Trends in International Franchise Laws* W4, ABA FORUM ON FRANCHISING (2008)

Andrew P. Loewinger and Thomas M. Pitegoff, Avoiding the Long Arm of the Law in International Franchising: Issues and Approaches W8, ABA FORUM ON FRANCHISING (1995)

Craig J. Madson and Katherine C. Spelman, *Similarity and Confusion in the Intellectual Property Arena* W11, ABA FORUM ON FRANCHISING (1997)

Christopher A. Nowak, John Pratt, and Carl E. Zwisler, *Franchising Internationally with Countries with Opaque Legal Systems* W20, ABA FORUM ON FRANCHISING (2006)

E. Lynn Perry and John L. Sullivan Jr., *Trademark Compliance and Enforcement Techniques* E/W12, ABA FORUM ON FRANCHISING (1992)

Marcel Portmann, *Franchising Sector Proves Global Reach,* in FRANCHISING WORLD (January 2007)

John Pratt and Luiz Henrique O. do Amaral, Civil Law for Common Law Practitioners (or How to Draft an Agreement for Use Overseas) W4, ABA FORUM ON FRANCHISING (2002)

Kirk W. Reilly, Robert F. Salkowski and Geoffrey B. Shaw, *Determining the Rules of Engagement in Litigation Here and Abroad* W5, ABA FORUM ON FRANCHISING (2008)

Catherine Riesterer and Frank Zaid, *Basics of International Franchising* L/B2, ABA FORUM ON FRANCHISING (1997)

W. Andrew Scott and Christopher N. Wormald, *Stranger in a Strange Land: Contrasting Franchising in International Expansion* W2, ABA FORUM ON FRANCHISING (2003)

Donald Smith and Erik Wulff, *International Franchising: The Unraveling of an International Franchise Relationship* 15/W13, ABA FORUM ON FRANCHISING (1993)

Frank Zaid, Pamela Mills, and Michael Santa Maria, *Essential Issues in International Franchising* LB/1, ABA FORUM ON FRANCHISING (2001)

II. Asian Resources

Stephen Giles, Andrew P. Loewinger, and Sherin Sakr, *Go East Young Franchisor: Franchising in Asia-Pacific Other Than China and India* W21, ABA FORUM ON FRANCHISING (2011)

Stephen Giles, *Franchising in Asia-Pacific Region, Who's Who Legal*: FRANCHISE 2012 (2012)

A. China

Ren Yanling, *Changes to Chinese Franchise Law: An improved Balance Between the Interests of Franchisors and Franchisees*, in INT'L JOURNAL OF FRANCHISING LAW 3 (2012)

China: New Franchsing Law, in Int'l Journal of FRANCHISING LAW 2 (2005)

Ella S.K. Cheong, *China*, in INTERNATIONAL FRANCHISING CHN/1 (Dennis Campbell gen. ed. 2011)

Yu Qin and Richard L. Wageman, *China*, in INTERNATIONAL FRANCHISE SALES LAWS China-1 (Andrew P. Loewinger and Michael K. Lindsey eds. 2010)

Mark Abell, Daniela C. Brito, and Paul D. Jones, *Franchising in the BRIC Markets (Brazil, Russia, India, and China)* W18, ABA FORUM ON FRANCHISING (2008)

B. Hong Kong

Andrea S.Y. Fong, *Hong Kong*, in INTERNATIONAL FRANCHISING HK/1 (Dennis Campbell gen. ed. 2011)

C. India

Preeti Mehta, *India—Termination of Master Franchise Agreements and the Consequences*, in INT'L JOURNAL OF FRANCHISING LAW 3 (2007)

Yoginder Pal, *Franchising in India*, FRANCHISING WORLD (October 2006)

Mark Abell, Daniela C. Brito and Paul D. Jones, *Franchising in the BRIC Markets (Brazil, Russia, India, and China)* W18, ABA FORUM ON FRANCHISING (2008)

D. Indonesia

Sigit Ardianto and Rivan F. Ramadhan, *Indonesia*, in INTERNATIONAL FRANCHISING INA/1 (Dennis Campbell gen. ed. 2011)

Rick Beckman and Ferry P. Madian, *Indonesia*, in INTERNATIONAL FRANCHISE SALES LAWS Indonesia-1 (Andrew P. Loewinger and Michael K. Lindsey eds. 2010)

Kendal H. Tyre, Jr. & Pierce Haesung Han, *The Ministry of Trade of Indonesia Limits Growth of Food and Beverage*

Franchises, NIXON PEABODY LLP: FRANCHISE ALERT (February 2013)

E. Japan

Takenari Shimizu, *Japan*, in INTERNATIONAL FRANCHISING JAP/1 (Dennis Campbell gen. ed. 2011)

Souichirou Kozuka and Takashi Kanai, *Japan*, in INTERNATIONAL FRANCHISE SALES LAWS Japan-1 (Andrew P. Loewinger and Michael K. Lindsey eds. 2010)

F. Malaysia

Leela Baskaran, *Malaysia*, in INTERNATIONAL FRANCHISING MAY/1 (Dennis Campbell gen. ed. 2011)

Mohd Bustaman Hj Abdullah and Wong Sai Fong, *Malaysia*, in INTERNATIONAL FRANCHISE SALES LAWS Malaysia-1 (Andrew P. Loewinger and Michael K. Lindsey eds. 2010)

Kendal H. Tyre, Jr. & Pierce Haesung Han, *Malaysian Government Actively Promotes Growth in Franchise Sector*, NIXON PEABODY LLP: FRANCHISE ALERT (October 2013)

Kendal H. Tyre, Jr. & Pierce Haesung Han, *Tapping Into Malaysia's Aggressive Franchising Goals*, PORTFOLIO MEDIA, INC.: LAW360 (November 2013)

G. Singapore

Daniel Lim, Bernard Lui, Michele The, and Vanessa Chew, *Singapore*, in INTERNATIONAL FRANCHISING SIN/1 (Dennis Campbell gen. ed. 2011)

H. South Korea

Brendon Carr and Jae-Hoon Kim, *South Korea*, in INTERNATIONAL FRANCHISE SALES LAWS South Korea-1 (Andrew P. Loewinger and Michael K. Lindsey eds. 2010)

Kendal H. Tyre, Jr. & Pierce Haesung Han, *South Korea adopts major amendments to the Fair Transactions in Franchise Business Act*, NIXON PEABODY LLP: FRANCHISE LAW ALERT (January 2014)

I. Taiwan

Wellington Liu and David Lu, *Taiwan*, in INTERNATIONAL FRANCHISE SALES LAWS Taiwan-1 (Andrew P. Loewinger and Michael K. Lindsey eds. 2010)

J. Thailand

Alan Adcock and Sriwan Puapondh, *Thailand*, in INTERNATIONAL FRANCHISING THA/1 (Dennis Campbell gen. ed. 2011)

K. Vietnam

Mai Minh Hang and Nguyen Anh Tran, *Vietnam*, in INTERNATIONAL FRANCHISE SALES LAWS Vietnam-1 (Andrew P. Loewinger and Michael K. Lindsey eds. 2010)

14932776.3

Printed in Dunstable, United Kingdom

91342631R00030